WE'RE NOT CRAZY, WE'RE TYPE A

BY

Krista Thornton, IHC

WE'RE NOT CRAZY, WE'RE TYPE A

Copyright © 2020 Krista Thornton, IHC

All rights reserved.

No part of this publication may be reproduced in any form, or by any means, electronic or mechanical, including photocopying, recording, or any information browsing, storage, or retrieval system, without permission in writing from the author, Krista Thornton, IHC.

ISBN:
978-1-7774644-0-0 (Paperback)
978-1-7774644-1-7 (eBook)

DEDICATION

To my mom who left this world too early to see that I turned out okay and all the trouble I gave her over the years was because of who I was and not because I wanted to create havoc for her.

To my children who shared, unknowingly, my life quest to understand why I often felt less than others, doubted myself and my abilities. Without you both, and the love I had for you, I'm unsure as to where I'd be today.

And to all Type-A's that have struggled with jobs, friends, emotions, mental health, substance abuse, health issues, relationships, and finding peace.

You too can learn to love being who you are. It is time to start celebrating what you bring into this world rather than always trying to be more!

FOREWORD

Many of us live our lives with little thought to our personality type, or how it affects the way we live. Yet, as Krista points out, personality types - and in particular Type-A – can have a profound effect, both on how we live, and how others perceive us.

Through clear explanation and real-life examples, this book takes us through the positives and negatives of Type-A personalities; their strengths and challenges, ups and downs. Authentic examples from Krista's own journey will help Type-A's make sense of sometimes confusing and frustrating behaviours that complicate their lives.

We live in a judgmental world, and adults who are thought to be 'outside the norm' in terms of behaviour sometimes need to be understood and accepted in order to lead a fuller and happier life. Advice for families and friends is also included here.

This book enables the Type-A personality to understand themselves and to move forward with acceptance, productivity, and happiness. If you are reading it, you are probably wondering about your own personality and its effect on your life and those around you. As you read, may you find some clarity and hope. And now the journey begins...

Susan Stacey, M.A.
Adult Educator and Author

CONTENTS

	AUTHORS NOTE	i
1	INTRODUCTION	1
2	PERSONALITY TEST	4
3	TRAITS OF A TYPE-A	8
4	PEOPLE, PLACES, THINGS	37
5	LIFE PHASES	51
6	HEALTH QUEST	55
7	RETIREMENT	59
8	TIPS TO LIVE & LOVE IT	60
9	RAISING A TYPE-A CHILD	67
10	CHILDRENS FEEDBACK	69
11	FINAL THOUGHTS	73

AUTHORS NOTE

What an adventure. Never in my wildest dreams did I think I would write a book. How very therapeutic to put into words what circles over and over again in your mind.

I don't have the secret to a happy healthy life. I'm not a doctor nor can I diagnose or recommend treatment. I understand that there is a place for western medicine. I don't have it all figured out. What I have written is a product of my experiences.

[You know there's a but here, don't you?]

But I know others are struggling to accept themselves: to find ways to enjoy their day to day lives, strive to understand how to make lasting relationships, and feel at peace with themselves. You are not alone in this battle and I hope to share some wisdom and experiences that may be helpful.

Start by congratulating yourself for beginning this self-journey! You have the right to be happy and choose what that looks like.

After all, this is your journey. Will you learn to love it or live with loathing it?

CHAPTER 1: INTRODUCTION

At last, I sat in a Psychiatrist's waiting room. I had graduated past the hundreds of hours with several psychologists, to a psychiatrist. I was a mess.

I avoided eye contact with the others who also sat in the waiting area hoping to find the mental health magic. I looked around and noticed the sterile environment of discomfort as I prepared myself to be told that I should go on some other kind of anti-depressants or anxiety medication. I was hoping it would be different, yet terrified that this doctor may prescribe something even more numbing than the last medication.

When the Psychiatrist entered the room, I couldn't help but notice how old he looked. What could he possibly understand about me? I was 35 at the time, had recently lost my best friend (my mom), was a single parent, and I was actively abusing substances to get by. I did however have enough wherewithal to realize I was spiraling down a dark hole. I would soon lose everything really important to me if I didn't figure out how to put my racing hamster wheel mind to rest.

So, I opened my mind as much as possible to listen to what this old doctor was about to say. He asked me a few questions about myself, much less than I expected, and then handed me a few photocopied pages. I saw that he had taken these from a book discussing personalities. It was at that moment that he introduced me to myself: Type-A!

I'd been in prison in my body and mind. In fact, I'm still learning to break free. I am adjusting to the understanding that it's a joyous lifelong journey that I can embrace or fight. It's for this reason that I decided to write this book. Those of you Type-A's know is an arduous task.

However, I know I'm not alone out there and my journey to find health and peace is one that I trust many Type-A's will relate to. My book offers insight so they too can learn to love their journey.

In my experience, being a Type-A personality offers some incredible strengths; grit, determination, competitiveness, drive, loyalty, desire to please, and many more, which eventually served me well. These strengths do however come at a price. For example, the inability to be happy with the here and now, always striving for more, looking for an imbalance when the balance is evident.

One of the most crippling is the need to be "perfect." The power of perfectionism is so strong that it shows up in many different ways. It tends to show itself through anxiety, panic, and acting out. Type-A's are constantly in search of something, anything, to feel perfect. I believe that this personality type is somewhat innate; however, it can also be hugely impacted by your childhood.

Unfortunately, when at a young age, you aren't aware yet as to why you continue to have this internal struggle and the impact it has on your everyday life. That is where the journey begins.

As time progresses, I'm learning how to keep my expectations in check and be grateful for all the here and nows. That way I enjoy all the blessings I have rather than continuing to search for more. Never mind discerning if the glass is half empty or half full. I've been consumed with always trying to fill it up. Now I'm finding ways to celebrate the glass half full.

Are you a Type-A? How has it unknowingly impacted your life? Your health? Do you want to love and accept who you are? How about some tips on how you can?

This book is intended to help you discover if you are a Type-A, or better understand a loved one who possesses this trait. It will also assist you in understanding how the different phases of our lives are impacted by our personality, the traits we benefit from and struggle with, and how we interact with people, places, and things in our lives. I will also discuss why this led me to a health quest and why it is very likely leading you there too.

Finally, I will share ways I overcame overwhelming situations in order to become better grounded.

I will feel very accomplished if you take a few tidbits away from this book that you can implement into a better life for you or someone you love.

CHAPTER 2: PERSONALITY TEST

Are you a Type-A or Type B?

It's important to keep in mind these two personality types reflect a spectrum and are being seen through my eyes – a Type-A woman.

Most people fall somewhere between the two extremes and men and women may experience them differently.

Additionally, there are not only two types of personalities in the world but for the purpose of this book, I will compare these two.

Typically, Type-A's have the following traits:

Do You…
- Like competition and will do almost anything to win?
- Find yourself cramming a lot into a day for fear of wasting time?
- Lack patience when delayed, especially in traffic?
- Need to be organized and like things in their place?
- Consider yourself ambitious and search for new things to learn?
- Find it difficult to turn off work, even on holidays?
- Find yourself multitasking often without realizing that you are?
- Constantly focus on your goals and finding ways to achieve them?
- Fear delays that may impact your success?
- Like to be the center of attention?
- Consume yourself with others' opinions of you?
- Get easily distracted?
- Become easily irritated and have a difficult time controlling it?
- Often feel stressed and overwhelmed?

WE'RE NOT CRAZY, WE'RE TYPE A

Words and phrases that will tend to motivate or get the attention of Type-A's:
- Here's the best way.
- Are you up for the challenge?
- Let's get it done!
- How fast can you get this completed?
- We are primarily focused on results.
- This is a competition.
- You've fallen into second place.
- Here's the bottom line.
- Can we hear your thoughts about…?

Dislikes and turnoffs of a Type-A:
- Dawdling.
- No one making a decision.
- Too many words without a point.
- Emails with multiple paragraphs.
- Explaining things more than once to the same person.
- Seeming weak.
- Being disorganized.
- Falling into routines.
- Feeling misunderstood.
- Being taken advantage of.
- Losing.
- Wasting time.

WE'RE NOT CRAZY, WE'RE TYPE A

Type-A's typically move at a pace twice that of most, becoming frustrated when we are held back by others. We find it extremely hard to sit and relax, since this feels like a waste of our time. Because we see our time as so valuable, to waste it seems catastrophic. When described by others, our speed and passion to complete tasks are often misinterpreted as impatience. Employers, however, see us as motivated to get the job done.

With the desire to complete tasks quickly, any roadblock is an invitation to start a new task. Which leads us to several tasks on the go at the same time. We rarely take the needed time to relax and re-energize, which sometimes pushes us to the brink of exhaustion.

We regularly criticize ourselves and our jobs. This is multiplied if we aren't able to complete all of the tasks we started, or didn't feel good about the job we did.

We are definitely our own worst enemy, rarely celebrating our successes without finding faults.

So, are you a Type-A?

How does this differ from a Type-B?

The Type-B personality is quite different than the Type-A personality. Those with Type-B personalities lean more towards being laidback. They can be described as relaxed and easygoing.

They usually:
- Focus on the small details around their work and assignments.
- Don't feel as stressed if all of their to-do lists don't get done.
- Can concentrate on one task until completion without the need to jump around.
- Like to take their time in the morning and dislike being rushed.
- Prefer creative ventures.
- Have philosophical thoughts.
- Are a quiet planner.
- Dislike dwelling on problems.
- Like a calmer pace to tackle chores or work.
- Become strong loyal friends.
- Require alone time.
- Opt for a quiet evening for celebrations.
- Like one-on-one interaction rather than large groups.

A Type-B person isn't always stress-free. However, they find it easier to manage their stress, especially in cases where their work may not get completed. This is a sure stressor for Type-A's that Type-B's seem to do ok with.

CHAPTER 3: TRAITS OF A TYPE-A

Let's have some fun and look at some traits and emotions of Type-A's. The good, the bad, and the ugly. I will then share tips on ways to learn to live with and love these traits. Perhaps some of the following personality traits are innate in nature, while others are nurtured throughout your life.

Living inside a Type-A body and mind:

~ Perfectionism ~

The desire to strive for flawlessness

This is the most dominant and debilitating trait of Type-A's. Perfectionists are self-critical in nature. "No not me! I don't need to be perfect." This was my first thought until I understood what it meant to be a perfectionist. The area that I mostly saw this in myself was in the critical aspect. I never believe I'm good enough at anything.

Type-A's will find everything that's wrong with what they've done rather than seeing what's great. We will hone in on imperfections and spot all mistakes. We are very judgmental of ourselves and others if we believe that failure has occurred.

I learned over time that perfectionism shows itself in many different ways:

Pushed by fear

Is it the thrill of the win that motivates you or the fear of losing?

Rather than being pulled by desire like high achievers, perfectionists are pushed by fear of not achieving them. Especially because nothing ever seems good enough and therefore no goal is actually ever reached.

All or nothing thinking

"If I can't be the best, I don't want to participate!"

This is the subconscious thought process when a Type-A is trying to decide on a plan of action. We set high goals and work hard toward them but won't accept almost perfect. So, we tend not to venture into areas that we aren't sure we can be the best.

Set unrealistic goals

When we set goals that are out of our reach, we set ourselves up for failure before even starting the task. "I want to lose 20 lbs in a week" or "I'm going to start exercising every day." Is this your post-holiday inner chatter?

Focused on results

Do you enjoy the journey or only see the destination? High achievers enjoy the process of working towards their goals. Type-A's only see the goal. We are so focused on either meeting it or the fear of not meeting it that we don't enjoy the process of growing and learning along the way.

Impacted by unmet goals

Do you get caught up on losses? Do you become consumed with a potential better way? Are you unable to let go, learn from it and move on?

Disappointment is a natural emotion. Type-A's will wallow in negative feelings and continue to beat themselves up for an unrealistic amount of time if they don't achieve their high expectations. This applies to themselves as well as if others disappoint them. They also have an impossible feat of faking how they feel when this happens as it becomes very apparent in their body language.

Defensiveness

Are you quick to rebut constructive feedback and see it as negative? Do you think it is intended to suggest you are a failure?

Since less than perfect performance is so hard for Type-A's to accept, we are defensive when given constructive criticism. We've already spent so much time beating ourselves up, often without merit, that we aren't able to see feedback as an opportunity to learn.

Well, that was a mouthful!

Perfectionism is very controlling and exhausting. Let me offer a few tips based on my own experiences; how I turned what could've been a downfall in my life and career into something worth loving.

TIPS TO OVERCOME PERFECTIONISM

Reformulating self-chatter

I have learned to hear my thoughts and challenge them. For example: "Wow, I'm fat" to "Wow, am I ever healthy" or "I'll never get this done" to "What's my next step?". Even if I don't believe what I'm telling myself, my brain starts to and I no longer have to think about the positive statement to follow the negative one. It automatically comes! As often said, "fake it 'til you make it!"

Celebrate the small wins

Are you consumed with a toothache when you have one? Heck yes! But do you celebrate when you don't have one? Not likely.

I now seek out what's going right, even small things such as the sun shining, I don't have any digestion issues at the moment, I had a successful bathroom break (Type-A's will get this one), and so on.

Make your own plans and satisfy your own needs

If others can't meet your expectations, then remove that barrier. I'm not saying let them off the hook, but I am saying don't think they can read your mind. For both of your benefits be direct about your expectations, or feel free to do it yourself. Their ultimate desire is your happiness.

Meditate

Are your ears up to your shoulders? Do you feel like you can't catch your breath? Is your head pounding out of frustration? You'll often hear me mention this.

Meditation works in many settings to offset a lot of otherwise difficult to manage situations. It's also the one that most Type-A's will say they can't do. "Meditate?!? Are you serious? Sit and do nothing for a long time? No can do!"

I too felt that way until I was pushed to do so (by my own fear of not fitting in) at a wellness retreat. I must say the first few times I tried, it was extremely painful. Looking for that measurement of success and feeling like I was failing.

We were silent in a room, sitting with our legs tucked under us. I wasn't sure what was more painful, the silence or discomfort of our position. I thought, are you kidding me? How could this possibly be good for me when everything is screaming "Yuck!".

I prevailed. I asked questions, researched, and found what does work for me in this area. Perhaps this will work for you too. I would suggest finding yourself a guided meditation online or an app that tells you what to do while meditating.

Don't have any expectations around success rate or length of time and simply focus on your breathing! I promise you, if nothing else, the ability to take five deep diaphragmic breaths will benefit you. It's a proven fact (since we love science) that this will help to reduce cortisol. Type-A's need Cortisol reduction!

Time to move on – enough about Perfectionism. One last thought, if you consider yourself a perfectionist, you can celebrate it. If I can simplify it to three types of people in the world: people that make things happen, people that let things happen, and people that say "What happened?". We all know where Type-A's fit in here. Perfectionism is not a fault, it is a trait; a strength. But a strength can become a weakness if left unchecked. Speaking of making things happen, the next trait we'll discuss is that of the "do'er".

~ Do'er ~

A person who completes various tasks with efficiency

When there's a job to be done are you first in line? Are you known as a hard worker? Do you prefer to know the end objective and go about it your way? Do you think about how to do something or just dig right in and get 'er done? Do you get frustrated knowing something needs to be done but the decision on the "what", is out of your control?

Type-A's are designed to take on tasks and get them done, usually in much less time than most. We prefer not to be told how it needs to be done but be given enough autonomy to do it ourselves. However, we don't always ask questions or read instructions and therefore sometimes end up in some peculiar situations.

TIPS ON HOW TO BEST BE A DO'ER

Be the doer that you are! Focus on the delivery and look to make partnerships with those that have mastered the attention to detail. Celebrate your partner every chance you get knowing they played a large part in the success you enjoy. If a partnership is not possible, I'd still forge forward and be prepared to listen and learn from any potential mistakes that may occur.

~ Competitiveness ~

A competitive person wants to be number one and finds it hard to be happy for someone else if they lose.

Do you see every task requiring multiple people as a competition? Is it all about the end result being a success for you? When is the drive to succeed too much? Has it provided the desired end result? Are you able to control this? Do you think you need to? Will you not push as hard if you don't believe you can win?

All of those questions are fair. As a Type-A, we constantly need accolades and exterior approval. Competitions provide this. There is a very clear winner, and we need it to be us. I wasn't even able to discern what it was for many years, but it was something I wasn't able to control. This was an area of my personality that eventually paid off. At first, it actually interfered with friendships because I wasn't able to be happy for others and would try to win at all costs. I preferred not to play competitive sports because my sister was so good, and I'd never match up. I acted out in school because my mind was not able to focus and therefore, I would not succeed. It was easier to be the bad kid and not be allowed to participate rather than compete knowing I couldn't succeed.

When I say it paid off, I mean it! I needed to find the niche that allowed me to be competitive and celebrate when I succeeded. Sales is one of these professions. Not one that most seek out, however, so I fell into sales much later in life. It didn't hurt that I had a manager who played on my desire to be #1, encouraging me to do more. She would make me aware when others surpassed my results knowing that it would make me want to sell more. Sales really is a career where you stand on your own to succeed or not. Does this mean you shouldn't be a team player? No, and I eventually became a great mentor as soon as I realized it too filled up my cup with accolades and praise. However, in a room of direct competitors there was always a bit I held back. Can't give away all your trade secrets now, can you?

If you think you are a Type-A and are at a point in your life where you are searching for a career to make you feel satisfied, I'd recommend the sales world or any job that similarly allows you the freedom to excel without a lot of rules and restrictions.

Tips on Putting
your Competitiveness to Work

Do what you love, let your passion drive you, and the competition will be fun. Force yourself to say the right things if you do not win and learn to mean them. This will help you make alliances with those that want to see you win too.

~ Anxiety ~

A feeling of worry and unease that's often a general overreaction to a situation that's not necessarily threatening. This emotion will often include physical sensations such as a racing heart, adrenaline rushes, difficulty breathing, fatigue, restlessness, and lack of focus.

Do you tend to catastrophize situations? Become easily distracted when things are out of your control? Are you unable to shut your brain off? Do you ever feel like someone is holding you by the throat making it hard to take deep breaths?

Anxiety, when improperly managed, can quickly turn into panic attacks. This is a feeling that you swear will make your heart explode as it beats so fast and so hard it rings in your head, seemingly ready to blow.

Anxiety shows itself in many different forms when you are a Type-A. My earliest memories are that of the codependency of my mom. When I wasn't with her, I often experienced anxiety or panic attacks. There were times when she had to pick me up from a friend's house in the middle of the night because of the state I was in.

Later in life, anxiety led me to act out and abuse substances to try and quiet my mind and get the constant attention I needed. Even to this day, now that I can understand and vocalize it, I know that my mind only shuts off when doing two things: drinking and participating in high-intensity exercise. Both allow me to feel a bit out of control for a short time. I can now knowingly decide how long that escape will be with a good understanding of the consequences should I fail to manage it wisely.

Tips on How to
Best Overcome your Anxiety

Meditate

Stop and take at least five deep breaths right into the bottom of your belly. You may need to start and stop this plan of action several times. I know it's not easy to calm a racing mind. First, invite the breath in and then push it out.

Manage your consumption of alcohol

Consuming alcohol can cause you to experience anxiety. If not at the time, the next day.

Exercise

Find an exercise that you love and that you can participate in regularly. This will assist you in shutting off your brain.

~ Panic attacks ~

Often follow poorly managed anxiety. Includes periods of severe fear with heart palpitations, shaking, gasping for air, and expecting something horrible to happen. The feelings can go from zero to unbearable in minutes lasting anywhere from a few seconds to hours.

Do you feel anxiety and panic arise when thinking about a particular situation? Can the consideration of something make you feel short of breath and heavy in the chest?

I experience panic attacks if I try to control my anxiety rather than feeling it and welcoming it in. As soon as I try to stop it, I invite a panic attack to start. My symptoms are like those above with the addition of adrenaline rushing through my body. This adrenaline serves as a warning telling me to find a bathroom, and quick.

The worst one I remember landed me in the hospital where, you guessed it, they gave me medicine. I was in Sweden at the time, so I relented to their recommendations out of fear of additional attacks. I spent the next several days of my vacation feeling like a Zombie.

Tips to Better Control Panic Attacks

Know your triggers and have an out

One of my triggers is feeling stuck in a room at bedtime with others. This could be friends or my spouse. If I don't feel I have the ability to get somewhere quiet and alone, I will eventually land in a full-on panic attack. When planning a trip or weekend away with friends, if there is any suggestion around me sharing a room without the ability to at least get to a couch or somewhere alone, then I instantly plant the scenario of panic in my mind. I've gotten up in the middle of the night when away with friends to rent another hotel room so that I could settle myself. Though I do feel that I've got this mostly in check now, I am always very aware of my options when these situations are presented to me.

You must be able to share your triggers. Be open and honest with the people you spend time with and ask questions in advance of committing to situations that will be uncomfortable for you.

Egg it on

When the anxiety starts, welcome it. Say, "Bring it on, give me what you got". This tends to diffuse the attack rather than if you try to stop it, which will likely bring it on full strength.

~ Uptightness ~

A state of being tense, nervous, unrelaxed, and tied up tight

This one is meant as comic relief. An interesting, semi-personal share with which I've recently been diagnosed. I'm curious to know if there are other Type-A's experiencing this. Being a Type-A and struggling to appropriately allocate the right amount of time for things, I spent my whole life trying to hurry my pee, pushing it so that I could be done with it fast. I mean, who's got time to sit on a toilet and relax? Come on, there are things to do!

What has that created for me? The inability to empty my bladder completely. I'm so uptight I've tied it up and now I always need to push to pee. I also need to pee again directly after peeing, especially if I had to hold it. Nuisance? Absolutely! I know where all the public bathrooms are in most countries I've visited. Rather than spending time exploring I spend time looking for the next bathroom. If you are reading this book and can relate, I'd love it if you'd come to my Pareto Wellness Facebook page and give me a "Yup! I get ya!!!".

On a more serious note, there are biomechanic physiotherapy practices that can teach you to relax and pee.

On a positive note, I don't need "laugh alots" like most ladies my age. Ain't nothing leaking through here!

~ Self Confidence ~

Believing enough in oneself that you are not impacted by what others think. You trust in your abilities to achieve what you desire.

I am not self-confident.

Unfortunately, because Type-A's are extroverts, many think we are the most confident people alive. Little do they know; we actually doubt ourselves regularly. We question our decisions over and over again to the point of not making one at times. We also get easily intimidated by others that are confident. We do not do well in contentious situations and will become flustered and unable to speak our minds.

In my sales career, I was often put in situations where the company I worked at was in question. Having a monopoly for several years meant that customer service hadn't been high on the radar and business owners would become angry. Rightfully so. However, I'd take this personally and find it almost impossible to defend. I'd be like an abused puppy, looking for a corner to hide in. I would ask myself, "I didn't do anything wrong, so why did it impact me?". If I was self-confident, I would have heard their concerns without emotion or ownership and tried to make it right. End of story!

Type-A's tend not to hear the words but instead, they feel them. They struggle with any situation that might mean they are not liked or unable to please.

In fact, it was my inability to be self-confident that pushed me to succeed. The more I succeeded, the more accolades I got and the more self-confident I believed I was. My self-confidence was defined by the exterior, not interior accolades.

Tips on How to Deal With your Self Confidence

Don't hide behind it. Be vocal with the fact that you aren't the self-confident person you appear to be. Allow those that matter inside. Help them understand you better by sharing your feelings. I'm married to a Type-B. He didn't really understand what a Type-A was until I was open with him. Surprisingly, years into our relationship, I shared with him that I looked for ways to help me shut off my brain. This was an alien statement to him that set him on a path to better understand the traits of Type-A. Now, he's my best advocate when it comes to understanding and accepting the person that I am. We all deserve that and should not be afraid to be open enough to let that in.

~ Monophobia ~

An extreme dislike of being alone or isolated

Have you been in senseless relationships? Tried to force them to work? Stayed involved longer than you should have but couldn't break it off? Found yourself dreading to go home to your empty house? Look for ways to fill your every moment? Find it difficult to sit and do nothing?

Monophobia is characterized by excessive reliance on other people for approval and a sense of identity. The problem here is that the fear of being alone may lead to co-dependency. Here are some traits of co-dependency that you should be aware of:

- Intense and unstable interpersonal relationships.
- Inability to be alone.
- Low self-worth.
- Fulfilling the needs of whom one is involved with before your own.

- Perfectionism.
- Feeling bored and empty.
- Need for acceptance and affection.
- Controlling of others.

They all seem to intertwine, don't they? This is one trait that's impacted by both nurture and nature.

I was raised by a stay-at-home Mom. She became my world at a very young age.

She filled up my cup whenever needed. It started a pattern of me needing one person in my life, rather than myself, to make me feel whole. Being Type-A stimulated this pattern and my relationship with my mom engrained it.

Tips to Manage your Monophobia

Force yourself to find time alone. I was usually pleasantly surprised when I did as it gave me peace that I wasn't aware I needed.

Make a list of what's important to you in a relationship and don't settle.

We are fortunate to live in a world that's brought us closer together by social platforms. So, if you find yourself alone, search for a group of individuals with similar interests. Perhaps you like to hike? Search for hiking groups. Use sites such as Meetup.com to meet others that may form part of your tribe.

Knowing you don't have to be alone but that you actively chose to, helps your mind welcome the idea.

~ Irritability ~

Feeling agitated, frustrated, and easily upset. Typically caused by a situation you perceive as being stressful, that often causes angry outbursts.

Do you have a short fuse? Do you find yourself getting

frustrated easily? Do you become angry in small situations?

I feel so irritated by simple things sometimes that I actually have self-chatter to force good decisions instead of bad. For example, sometimes when I'm putting the dishes away and feeling irritable, I have to tell myself to put the glasses in the cupboard instead of throwing them across the room.

I've discovered one thing I do to try and relax is also one thing that heightens my irritability – drink. Alcohol is not a good thing for a Type-A. Though it may feel like a fix at the time, it absolutely backfires.

Does this mean that I've learned my lesson and quit drinking? Absolutely not! As a Type-A, all or nothing does not work. If I was to obsess about whether or not I should drink, I'd want to drink more. Instead of abstinence, I bargain the when's and how's with myself. Then I set up the right framework for the aftermath to deal with the irritability that will surely come.

Tips to Better Manage Irritability

Know your triggers

Your first priority should be to understand what sets you off. When possible, avoid situations that cause you to be irritable. One of my triggers is traffic, an easy workaround for the most part.

Understand your limits

Should you decide a drink or two is the route you want to go to ease irritability, I suggest you have a few drinks early in the evening to get that relaxing buzz, then turn to water before going to bed. As long as you fall asleep without the buzzing feeling you shouldn't wake up with lingering irritation.

Please know that I do not encourage alcohol as a form of self-medication but thought I'd share how I have managed it over time.

Exercise

If you are feeling irritated, try and go for a walk or participate in whatever form of exercise helps you get the brain break you need. The movement will stimulate the happy hormone, serotonin, which will help offset the irritability.

Meditate

If it's situational, remove yourself and take five deep breaths! A short but sweet meditation will often work.

Practice gratitude

When I'm feeling irritated, I look at the things I am grateful for. It's very hard to be irritated, anxious, or angry when in a state of gratitude. Keep a gratitude journal nearby, write and/or read regularly.

Theanine

Another thing I've tried is a natural product called Theanine. It does exactly what it says it will do. It helps to calm your mood.

Side note: I do not like to take anything too often as it decreases in effectiveness over time and may affect the production of natural helpful substances our bodies make. I prefer to use this method as a last resort after I've exhausted all my other means to relax.

~ EQ vs IQ ~

EQ - Emotional Quotient allows you to feel what you say or hear and control how you react to it. IQ - Intelligence Quotient is derived from different tests designed to assess your intelligence.

Do you act based on fact or do emotions play a role in your decisions? Will you make decisions contrary to others because it feels good? Do you take rejection personally? Do you find it hard to be logical when you feel emotionally attached?

Type-A's tend to score low on the EQ scale. We struggle to keep our emotions in check. This doesn't mean we are not intellectual, but it does mean that we feel more than most.

TIPS TO DEVELOP YOUR EQ AND IQ

Work towards a balance of these. Too much of either will be seen as a turn-off. In a professional situation, logic (IQ) needs to play a role. However, I don't believe it always has to be dominant at the expense of not showing your EQ. This is an area we could explore immensely. I would encourage you to do more reading around this to grasp a better understanding on the impact it has.

EQ can be an amazing trait, especially, if you are in a role where emotions are appreciated – it shows you are genuine. However, keeping it in check and using it appropriately will work more in your favor. Controlling EQ is not an easy task for Type-A's. It's a work in progress for me. Understanding the difference and how to effectively use both is the first step.

~ Controlling ~

The need to be in control and dominate situations and people. Often Type-A's will be labeled control freaks.

Do you need to tell someone how to drive? Can't participate in something if you aren't in charge? Do you feel sorry for yourself because no one plans anything for you? Do you question others' decisions if different than yours?

The need to be in control is practically out of our

control. We say we want to relent and let others take over, but we don't even know-how to do this.

This trait works well in some careers. It was paramount during a sales call. I was always organized to the tee and, as long as I had a welcoming client that allowed me to stay on task, all went well. However, if I was challenged, I was easily thrown.

My need for control didn't always make me the best team player, but it usually made me number one.

TIPS FOR CURBING YOUR NEED TO CONTROL

For your career. Look for work that puts you in a decision-making position. Practice phrases that help you achieve what you want but that empowers your people's input. Knowing our weaknesses and celebrating others that have our backs, rather than trying to do it all, will work miracles. If you find it impossible to let go of the reins, find a mentor you respect and who achieves this and ask them to work with you. Then you must be open to feedback. Know that weaknesses are actually areas of opportunity!

When it comes to relationships, this is a trait we need to be very mindful about. Trying to control the people we love will eventually come at a price. Learn to bite your tongue or find a tone in which you can make your recommendation without sounding bossy and controlling. Ask your significant others how they'd like to be spoken to and practice, practice, practice until it becomes second nature. Be the first in your relationship to make things great and if you are with the right one they too will jump on board.

~ Digestion issues ~

Acid reflux, indigestion, excessive burping, and flatulence…

Do you experience any or all of these? Have you succumbed to the doctor's suggestion of taking acid reflux medication or are you constantly chewing Tums or swallowing Pepto Bismol?

Stress plays such a large role in our digestion. Type-A's live in a constant state of stress. A stressed body resides in the sympathetic nervous system. This system is prepared for a fight or flight response, which served us well during the times that we either had to catch our food or it caught us. Now, however, it increases unnecessary cortisol in our body, having a huge impact on our digestive system. If we can get out of the sympathetic side and into the parasympathetic side, then our bodies can rest and digest. In doing so, our body uses our food's nutrients to nourish us, aiding in our digestion.

How, you might ask? Let's start with the fact that Type-A's don't usually slow down long enough while they're eating for the stomach to realize food is about to enter. Who's got time to be quiet and enjoy the food we are about to eat? Let's just get it done and move on!

As we age, our digestion slows down all on its own, so we need to offset this by giving it half a chance and doing our part to assist it by implementing some of the tips below.

Tips on Improving your Digestion

Slow down

Not easy right? Practice mindful eating. Make your meals look fancy so that you want to enjoy every bite like you would if you were at a restaurant.

Put your fork down between every bite rather than shoveling one forkful after another.

Avoid talking while eating

Or at the very least, talk only when your fork is resting on your plate. Finish whole sentences before picking that fork back up.

Try not to eat on the run or while doing something else

Take time to sit and celebrate your food. Eat when you are eating, nothing else, just eat! Emails, messages, and social media apps, etc. can all wait.

Avoid irritating foods

If you are unsure which foods give you grief, I'd recommend a 21-day elimination diet to find out. They will be "bio-individual" (unique to you) so don't assume what they are. This type of program will start by removing all typical digestive irritants and add them back in one at a time. Trust me, if you give your body half a chance, it will tell you loud and clear what it's struggling with. Then you have a choice to make.

If you are doing all of these things and would like a bit more support, I have great results with digestive enzymes[1]. If you are interested in knowing more about these, let's chat.

~ Insomnia ~

A disorder resulting in the inability to fall asleep or stay asleep

Insomnia often leads to daytime sleepiness, irritability, and lack of energy; it can also cause a feeling of depression.

Though sleeplessness is not exclusive to Type-A's, we as a group generally struggle to turn our minds off.

Do you lay in bed at night and evaluate your life? Do you think about what you did or didn't do that day? Do you beat yourself up for things from the past? Do you try to plan out the rest of your life? Do you worry about not falling asleep and therefore stay awake?

This has been a plague for me off and on my whole life. As a child, I remember dealing with anxiety when I was unable to fall asleep before my mom did.

Later in life, my abuse of drugs and alcohol played havoc on my normal sleeping patterns to the point where I found myself depending on Gravol, sleeping pills, or nighttime cold medicine to try and nod off. I'd often find myself watching the clock 'til the wee hours of the morning.

As we age, we lose sleep worrying about things that are entirely out of our control… our kids' well-being, our health, and even our own death.

Tips to Battle Insomnia

Practice a nighttime ritual

This could mean adjusting the time you go to bed as well as better structuring what you do before bed. Try to respect it seven days a week!

Eliminate technology

Try to put your electronics away at least 30 minutes before hitting the hay to allow your thoughts to be yours and not those that have been stimulated by the online world.

Exercise

Exercising allows your body and mind to match in fatigue. I'd highly recommend you find some kind of activity that works for you so that you will make it a part of your routine. (Try to avoid doing this too close to bedtime as it may have an adverse effect.)

Talk to a naturopath

Perhaps you have too much cortisol in your body to nod off properly. There are cortisol reducers you could consider trying under the advisement of a naturopath.

Read

Read a mindless book that allows you to escape your current reality but doesn't force you to concentrate too much.

Meditate

Once again, I encourage you to find an online guided meditation that you can follow. I use the platform called GAIA. It offers several nighttime meditations to help you relax and fall off to sleep.

All that said, I still struggle to fall asleep easily and inner chatter is required so that I don't invite in anxiety or panic attacks. So, I tell myself things like "It doesn't really matter if I fall asleep right away, it's all good". I also force myself to take deep breaths knowing that this state of relaxation is almost equivalent to sleep. These deep breaths help me to stop thinking about perfecting sleep and enjoy what I'm experiencing at that moment.

Finally, I do have sleeping pills as a security blanket. I take them with me, especially when going on trips. If my mind is already spinning and showing signs of anxiety in advance of going to bed, I don't mess with it. I take a ½ of a pill before starting on my other routine bedtime rituals. Once again, I do this knowing that if I try fighting it, I will likely end up regretting it.

It is important to note that I don't support or encourage pharmaceutical drugs as a first response. There are too many possible negative side effects that will eventually catch up to us.

I also think it's important to note that they will not continue to be a successful plan of action should they become the norm. Your body will adjust to them, forcing you to take more for the same effect. I want medication to work when I have no alternatives left, so I use it sparingly. I'd suggest the same for you.

WE'RE NOT CRAZY, WE'RE TYPE A

~ Racing minds ~

The inability to shut off your brain; thoughts constantly stream in and may become manic

Do you have multiple thoughts in your mind at the same time? Will you be talking about one thing and switch gears quickly noticing something new? Do songs play over and over again in your mind? How about counting letters in a word of a sentence and trying to force them to fit into your lucky number, without impacting it phonetically?

As I've aged, I now repeat stories that I've recently experienced and want to share in just moments to my husband or daughter over and over in my mind.

It's like I'm practicing what I'm going to say. Sometimes it's overwhelming. It's as if I'm going to forget something that just happened or that I'll use too many words if I don't decide exactly what I'm going to say.

From what I understand, this is a form of meditation. It forces a controlled thought over and over in our minds eliminating multiple thoughts to resolve.

TIPS TO LIVE WITH YOUR RACING MIND

One tip – Invite it in and let it happen! Know that it's your mind's attempt at trying to settle. Also, know that it's a part of who you are, and trying to quiet it unnaturally will cause you anxiety.

Practice what we already discussed to help us relax and ease our minds. Exercise, meditation, and redirection to something you love.

~ Passion ~

Interests and desires providing a considerable amount of pleasure that are acted on with intensity

Do you become easily excited and are often accused of being aggressive about something you believe in? Does your voice get elevated and your actions more distinct? Is your passion confused for control? If you found something you were passionate about and then it was removed from your life, what impact did that have?

I'm not sure I knew how passionate I was until I fell into what became my career. As mentioned, I believe that sales' is one of the best careers for Type-A's. Being in sales allows us the ability to receive the exterior accolades that are so important for us. In saying that, it can, however, mask the inability to find inner contentment.

Passion is a positive trait of Type-A's that can be misused and misunderstood if not recognized and appreciated.

Tips to Loving your Passionate Side

Don't let anyone dampen your passion. It's what makes us unique and exciting. However, be mindful and content with the fact that not everyone shares your passions.

Work towards a delivery that is assertive rather than aggressive. I, a fellow Type-A, understand that your heightened excitement comes from a good place. Others may not.

~ Guilt ~

Guilt is an emotion we feel when we believe we are responsible for a particular outcome that has violated what's considered morally or ethically acceptable.

Do you beat up on yourself if you've had an extra cookie? Do you get down on yourself if you don't get a project done? Do you hear yourself saying "shoulda, coulda, woulda"?

Guilt is the thief of joy! Living by "What if's" instead of "What are's" will rob you of your happiness. Spending unnecessary time worrying about things that happened in the past or might happen in the future and missing out on what's happening now will also do that. I'm not saying don't plan for the future, but make sure you do so without missing out on the present.

TIPS TO OVERCOME YOUR GUILT

Modify your self chatter

When you have a guilty thought, you must repeat out loud what the reality is. If you did not cause this to happen then don't accept ownership of it. If you are responsible, then uncover the lesson you are to learn and move on.

Ruminating gets you nowhere.

~ Worry ~

A worrywart is a person who worries excessively, especially about unimportant matters.

Do you ever lay in bed at night feeling sick to your stomach, worrying about dying? I literally mean a right-down-in-the-bottom-of-your-belly sick feeling. You know you have no control over it, but it doesn't stop you from worrying. How about when your children first start to drive or meet their first boyfriend… do you worry about accidents or about their hearts getting broken? Do you have stories conjured up in your mind that are so vivid you dream them? How about worrying so much about what someone thinks of you that you aren't able to act yourself when around them?

I remember my days as a Weight Watcher leader when I would have 80 members or more enjoying my lecture. You'd think I'd feel good, right? But wait – I thought I saw someone that rolled their eyes or didn't look as interested as the others. I'd focus most of my attention on impressing that one person. Why? If I worry about what they think will it make a difference in my life or theirs? What about all the others that were enjoying the meeting? Was I not being unfair to them in worrying about the one who wasn't?

This is a tough one that I still find myself doing regularly. I am, however, very aware of it now and take immediate steps to cut it off at the pass.

TIPS TO BETTER ADDRESS YOUR WORRIES

Modify your self chatter

Once again, modifying your self-chatter is really the most efficient way to manage your worrisome thoughts. Changing ourselves is not the aim, learning to love and accept ourselves is.

~ Planner's Mentality ~

Do you find yourself planning every event to the last detail? Have you ever been frustrated after letting someone else do the planning and it did not turn out as you expected? Do you become consumed with what's next in your plan and often miss out on what's happening now?

Planners are not content to waste time which is why they actively and responsibly fill their schedules with "must-dos" and "gotta-get dones". This can be as positive as it can be negative. As they say: "failing to plan is planning to fail". So, I do plan, sometimes to a fault.

Type-A's like to make plans since it will allow them to know what to expect. However, if we ever want others to plan things for us, we have to let them do so and keep our expectations in check if it's not exactly what we were hoping for. Depending on your situation, planning it all yourself may feel more comfortable and less stressful for you. However, let me warn you that too much planning can cause you to miss out on the now.

I've been fortunate to do a considerable amount of international travel with my hubby. Often it wasn't until I was home, either looking at pictures, or telling someone about the trip, that I realized how amazing it was.

When my children were 9 and 11, I planned a trip to Disney World. After spending hours on the phone (the Internet wasn't a thing back then) I had every moment of our 10-day vacation planned. Once on vacation, we rushed from one spot to the next trying to make sure we met all of the obligations I had set for us. Funnily enough, my very active, unable-to-tire child, looked at me after day 3 and said: "Mom, can we just chill tonight please?".

TIPS TO LIVE IN THE NOW

Make a point of stopping, looking around, and saying: "Wow!" at every chance. Try to take time and smell the roses. Sometimes what comes from not planning is an experience you'd never have thought to plan. Go ahead and let go of the reins and see where things lead you. Allow yourself to feel a little uncomfortable with the process as it may surprise you.

~ Fearing Judgment ~

Placing too much importance on what others think often consumes us. Why? Others may judge, but so do we. Do what others think of us have an impact on our lives? Nope! In fact, what others think of us is none of our business.

You will find your tribe. Those are the people that will love you no matter what. One great thing about getting older is that you realize no one outside your tribe really gives a sh!t about you. The person you need to answer to is inside of you.

Seek out people who make you feel good about yourself. The beauty of the world is that we are all different. There's nothing better than people watching to realize how true that is. As long as you aren't being mean to others, allow them to judge away. In fact, it can be really fun to give them something to talk about.

TIPS ON UNDERSTANDING JUDGMENT

Look inwards. Do you judge? You likely do. Simple thoughts about others are judgments. Don't become consumed with what you believe others think about you. At the end of the day, what does it change in your life?

~ Assertiveness ~

The ability to get your point across or ask for what you want without being aggressive

Do you approach situations with directness? Does this cause others to shy away? Do you respect others' opinions or try to convince them that you're right? Do you ask questions and reward them for proper understanding? Do you accept and appreciate other points of view?

If you take an aggressive approach you are being hostile in nature. An assertive approach, on the other hand, is direct in a way that is respectful of others. Type-A's can struggle to find the balance between being assertive and aggressive.

We don't intentionally mean to offend but we believe strongly in our opinions and kick into competition mode when we want to convince others of something.

If while being passionate you are assertive, that's great. However, be aware of how your information is being received. If you push too hard, one of two things will happen: others will relent, or the discussions will become heated.

TIPS TO MASTERING ASSERTIVENESS

Ask questions! Once you really understand others' point of view, feel free to share yours. Be open with the fact that you become very passionate and that it may appear to be pushy.

Above all else, don't lose your passion and excitable ways, just find ways to communicate them favorably to others.

This is not necessarily an inclusive or exclusive list of traits or emotions of Type-A's. They are however a list of the ones that I personally deal with regularly. If you do too, I hope you've had a little chuckle and found a few helpful nuggets.

Let's move on to discuss how Type-A's interact with people, places and things.

CHAPTER 4: PEOPLE, PLACES, THINGS

Let's continue by exploring how Type-A's deal or interact with these.

PEOPLE

Type-A's want everyone to like them. They will often change the way they are to try and suit whomever they are spending time with. It's never done in malice; however, it is recognized by the people who really love them.

Type-A's don't do well with perceived awkward silence in a group setting. For that reason, they will often control the conversation and talk a lot to avoid that. They will also be the clown of the crowd if it's giving them the attention they desire, even if people are laughing at them rather than with them. We are often invited to parties to entertain.

However, this trait impedes our ability to create meaningful relationships as we spend too much time talking and not enough time listening. Relationships can only be built when sharing information from both sides. This is true because everyone loves to talk about themselves and be made to feel proud of the person they are. Often, Type-A's are too busy entertaining or talking about themselves which often leaves a new connection feeling rather empty.

WE'RE NOT CRAZY, WE'RE TYPE A

At the age of 23, I went to Université Laval to learn to speak French. When trying to make friendships, I struggled. Being new to an area and with no existing friends, I felt the need to attract the wrong kind of attention in an attempt to make new relationships. At the time, I couldn't understand why they didn't invite me to shop or events that were not party-centric. It was not until much later in life that I realized they really only wanted me around to entertain and make a fool of myself. Outside of party situations, however, they likely found me obnoxious and abrasive.

Type-A's don't intend on being obtrusive, quite the contrary. What we are really trying hard to do is be liked by everyone (which we all know is a recipe for failure!). Those that know we are genuine and give us a chance soon learn how insecure we are and thus the reason for the outbreaks. They also learn how giving, loyal and kind we are. If they don't get the chance to know us on that level, then they won't seek out our company. They either love us or hate us. Very few are neutral.

My dad was a true testament to this. He was actually very obnoxious in some situations. To the point that I too had a difficult time being around him. Especially when he was drinking, he'd say things at all costs to get a reaction, good or bad. Typical Type-A attention seeker.

Several nights we'd leave the golf club that my dad thought would make us better people (tongue and cheek) and stop at the Chinese restaurant on the way home to soak up some of his booze. Much to my mom's chagrin, she was usually the driver. Tung Hing was his favorite. Meat egg rolls and Wor Shel Guy. When the waitress would approach, he'd say "I love taking pregnant women home". After a very odd look, the waitress would respond that she wasn't pregnant. Dad would say "you're not home yet either". He'd then often call her something flattering like a "Blue-eyed hooker". Sounds appalling, doesn't it? All while my dad and my older sister would laugh their asses off, Mom and I would sink into our chairs with embarrassment. There were several occasions and off-kilter phrases my dad would say, typical uncontained Type-A behavior.

Although these traits were ingrained in me both through nature and nurture, as I matured, I realized they were not patterns I wanted to repeat.

Mom passed 22 years in advance of my dad. Unfortunately, his new wife pushed out most of his friends, children, and grandchildren. Because of this, during his last days, he shared his belief with me that only a few people would be at his funeral. Sad isn't it? That at the age of 78, my dad didn't feel understood or loved by the people who were in his life for so long. Wow, was he wrong! So even though he was direct, obnoxious, and downright embarrassing at times, he had a heart of gold and touched a lot of people. The church was full!

Type-A's like to be surrounded by people, not always fans. We think the bigger the show the better the fun; and though it stops our minds from racing for a little while, it also gives us lots of material to worry about after the fact. We replay the event over and over in our minds several times until we are definitely convinced that we did something wrong. I'll sometimes find myself apologizing for things, not even sure why.

Type-A's don't have the same filter as most. We don't see things as private in our lives as others do. What's in our heads usually comes out of our mouths. This can create real relationship issues with some. When I was younger, I couldn't keep a secret to save my life. I also had a really tough time knowing what my friends wanted me to share and what they wanted to be kept private. Eventually, I realized this and would ask, is this private? Is this between you and me or can I share this news? My life has pretty much always been an open book. Good, bad, or indifferent.

Relationships

A real necessity for a Type-A. We dislike solitude. However, when it's beyond our control, and we find ourselves alone, we quite like it. It's not something we seek out. We generally think the more the merrier.

Type-A's will often stay in a relationship well beyond its best before date. Our insecurities make us stay even if we aren't happy, for fear of being alone. I've tried to put a square peg in a round hole several times – the relationship was doomed but I still tried to force it to work.

After the end of my first marriage, I decided I needed a new one. I wasn't prepared or seemingly able to just be on my own. Plenty of Fish, an online dating site, seemed to be the route at that time. It quickly became my obsession, my project. I had to find Mr. Perfect and quick. Being an assertive gal, I didn't have any trouble getting first dates. I power planned them. There were days that I'd meet a guy for coffee, another for lunch, and finish off the day with dinner with a third. Going through the same list of interview questions for the right guy. Probably one of the most disheartening times of my life! Nothing felt natural about any of my meetings. I was so direct and needy that I intimidated most of them. The most difficult thing was accepting the fact that not everyone liked me. Most times I wasn't even me – I was trying to be who I thought they wanted me to be.

I was also looking for a mirror image of myself. Someone that loved everything I did and that wanted to achieve similar things – another Type-A, I thought. When I think back on that now, I realize that two Type-A's in a relationship is a means for a disaster. We really need a Type-B to help calm us and accept us the way we are. Another Type-A would simply compete and power struggles would prevail.

With friend relationships, female Type-A's seem to struggle more than men. Women tend to compete even if they don't know each other. This is heightened with a Type-A gal because of our outward ways. Albeit genuine and giving, others will be intimidated and jealous. We take this on and worry about them liking us or not. It's a real shame we give this power to anyone.

Growing up, I tended to be very protective of the relationships I had. It was important to me that I had one steady friend to interact with and unknowingly control. I wasn't keen on them interacting with others. I'd become angry and verbally abusive should they spend time with anyone else and not include me. I know I lost friends over the years because of this. I've realized that the harder I try to make someone like me, the less energy I have to give to the ones that really do.

This truly is the point of this book – creating awareness and learning how to give attention to the things that directly impact our life or the life of those that we love.

Mom was always there for me and became my best friend as I grew. I abused her love and loyalty terribly as a youngster, but she never gave up on me. I acted out as most Type-A's do. Fortunately, I had the chance to make all that up to her before she passed. We became inseparable as I matured. I was always confused by others that didn't have the same relationship with their moms. She was my everything – my rock, my cheerleader.

She too often doubted herself, thinking she wasn't good enough of a person. I wasn't aware of this until her dying days when I learned she carried for an incredibly long time, the guilt of her mom passing alone. Sadly, she didn't feel warranted to share her emotions and get the healing she deserved. She passed at the age of 54 from a brain tumor. Some believe we can create our own disease. That it will fester where we give it attention. My mom spent years dealing with a grief that she blamed herself for. Then to die from a primary brain tumor at a time that they were very rare is telling.

In many ways, my mom was my soulmate. Odd, but true. This of course did not allow me to look for or develop the relationship with a man the way I should have. When I learned of my first pregnancy, it was my mom I thought to tell, not my husband.

In hindsight, our relationship was built on another one of my projects, I felt it was time to have a family and he was to be the dad. My mom approved of him which fired my quest.

Once Mom passed, my marriage went to pieces. I expected this man that had never been given the chance to be my soulmate to step up to the plate and fill the hole left by my mom's death. Although our marriage didn't prevail, fortunately, Mom was right about him. He's maintained a very healthy relationship with me, our kids, and even my new husband.

Thinking back on my professional relationships, early on in my career, there were some growing pains. Being a sales organization, jealousy reared its ugly head. Those that didn't do as well as I, were always looking for possible mishaps, things I was doing unethically. Rather than giving me the benefit of the doubt that I had finally found a job that really fit my Type-A personality.

Eventually, I proved myself and was blessed to develop some amazing lifetime friendships through this career. Those that gave me the chance realized how passionate, compassionate and genuine I was.

My desire to lift others up and be their mentor was satisfying and beneficial to us all. To this day, I've maintained those friends and miss our regular interactions terribly. These ladies have all taught me so much about myself and helped me become a better person.

Although a tough exterior, Type-A's want to evolve and learn personally from others that we love and trust. We are very open about our frustrations and look for friendly feedback.

Allow me to share a few of these tips, perhaps they'll help you as well. I cannot take credit for these ones.

I once had a very difficult boss; it was later in my career and it was threatening everything I had worked so hard to become. A friend, I'll call her "Gal A", would allow me to vent, and when I was done she'd say, "Krista, there is a lesson to be learned from this relationship. Once you've learned it, she'll be gone, and you'll be better for it. For now, place yourself inside a beautiful bubble, and don't let her pierce it. Allow her words and actions to bounce off." She was indeed correct; I survived and am now happily retired from the career I so loved, on my terms, not hers.

"Gal B" would also allow me to ramble on about my frustrations, often in my quest to understand the man I love dearly. Women have the tendency to voice their frustrations to each other about their mates. Even more so by Type-A (non-private gals) which, of course, is fine since we just want to be heard.

This beautiful lady taught me if you are always focused on the things you don't like, that's all you'll see, spend more time celebrating all the things you love, and you'll get more of just that. Additionally, with work situations, working for a business in total transformation, there were lots of frustrations. She'd allow me to vent for a while, as would she, and then she'd stop and say: "What are some solutions?".

I so love both of these ladies for their words of wisdom that will forever mark my life. There are a few others that have also impacted how I think and feel.

"Gal C", I had the pleasure of interviewing for a job. Considerably younger than I, so I felt as though I'd be the one in charge. After all, I would be her boss; I'm the one doing the hiring here. Turns out, I was not the interviewer as planned; she led the time we spent together and had me selling her on why she should come work for me. I saw myself in this smart young lady. A fellow Type-A. Determined to succeed and not afraid to ask for what she wanted. So, I hired her, of course. Another lifelong friend.

"Gal D", a sister friend from the age of 15. I shared several life changes with this gal. Words of wisdom she imparted to me that I still use to this day: "When you are deciding who you will spend time nurturing in your life relationships, think of this: how do they make you feel <u>about</u>

you, not how do they make you feel?". Think about the difference here, it's huge!

Last but not least, my best buddy during my single-mom years and to this day. She was there for me in so many ways. My Plus 1 at many work incentives trips. My confidante during my Mr. Right project. As well, my handy lady extraordinaire. She accepts me for all my good and bad ways and our personalities gel beautifully. She is such an inspiration to me. She not only knows how to bake, sew, garden, and cook, she can also plumb, paint, lay hardwood floors, tile, and weld. She even built and raced her own stock cars! A perfect buddy for a Type-A. I continue to be grateful for the special moments I spend with her.

The most life-changing relationship I've had is with my current husband/friend/partner. He's allowing me to become who I truly am. I believe we continue to learn about ourselves. With the right relationship, we also realize how we can impact this wonderful life we are living. His support and desire to truly understand me as a Type-A is amazing. When I first met this fella, I was surprised that he'd want to be with me. He's so confident, kind, and loving with the people he calls friends and family. His ability to assess a situation and remain in control was odd to me. I, on the other hand am easily shook, cranky, bossy, and needy. As I got to know him better, after initially trying to sabotage what we were developing, I realized most of the people in his life were also Type-A's. He enjoys these relationships as they balance him out. He doesn't require what I do from situations. Thankfully securing a very powerful, accepting, connection. Never have I been with someone that truly wants me to be happy the way he does. He makes me feel sexy, beautiful, and loved! I'm very blessed to have this man in my life. As he always reminds me, nothing is perfect, but it sure feels pretty close.

I sincerely apologize to any that have also impacted my life but that have not been given space in my book. Trust me when I say that I am forever grateful to you all. I know

I'm not an easy person to love so if you've made space for me in your life, thank you!

Family

Family is interesting amongst Type-A's. When we're young, we don't want much to do with our family as we prefer to act out and don't appreciate that it doesn't fit in with their rules. We're indifferent that they are worried about our lives. We do, however, find our way and realize the importance of those who love us. When that happens, we can't do enough for them. Especially those special few that stood by us through it all and gave us the time to spread our wings and figure things out.

My Type-A dad was raised by abusive parents. Because of this, he tended towards a very direct, old-school disciplining approach. He thought he had to be tough. I remember getting the belt from Dad and I swear to this day it hurt him more than me. I too found this when raising my own kids. We want to be stern, but we are actually so soft inside that it's very painful for us. Dad never shared this with me but learning more of myself as a Type-A, I now understand him better. He spoke a tough track but often didn't follow through. His bark was worse than his bite. As a child, I thought it was because Mom played interference. Now, I think he counted on that.

My non-Type-A Mom was the disciplinarian; her favorite weapon was the wooden spoon. I, being a Type-A, always in control, unable to show emotions, didn't succumb to her punishment. Her style was not effective on me. I would not let her know it hurt me until she left the room, and I could do so in private. Not giving her the satisfaction to see how much it impacted me. It was definitely more mentally than physically painful.

I needed my mom's affection and attention. Whether it was positive or negative. I was her Velcro child. It was the beginning of me needing one person in my life to share everything with. I had a tough time making and keeping friends because I either wanted to control them and their time or did things they knew were wrong and weren't prepared to participate in.

Once we have our own families and see how our traits are transferred, we then start to better understand ourselves. We will explore what it's been like raising a Type-A child a bit later in this book. As you will see, Type-A's interact best with other personality types, not always so well with other Type-A's, even in their family. We love them and understand them, but it does make for an oil and fire interaction when times are spent together.

PLACES

Type-A's are more about experiencing a place rather than seeing it. Driving around seeing how lovely things look and spending hours in a vehicle is a sure way to stress us out. If we are aware of the end destination and are excited about what's waiting for us, we find ways to cope. One of the best inventions for Type-A's are tablets. Wi-Fi or not, we can play, read, or peruse information we have stored. In fact, we will often download a game and become the very best at it, shortly thereafter tiring of it and moving onto the next. Fortunately, in this day and age, there are tons of games to monopolize our time. However, since we also live in a constant stress state where cortisol is firing around in our veins, technology is actually counter-intuitive to our health, so balance is paramount.

When traveling, we prefer to have it all planned in advance so that we know how to best prepare mentally and physically. However, when things are not as expected, we usually can't hide our disappointment. Our faces and body language tell all.

We don't like to arrive early to whatever event we have as we dislike waiting. It seems like such a waste of time and therefore added stress. Because we try to plan everything to the exact moment, when something interrupts our flow, we become very agitated and angry. We end up rushing around to get to places on time. Road rage is a very natural occurrence for us. We are rushing to arrive right on time, so we rarely enjoy the journey.

THINGS

Type-A's are often about quantity, not quality. This doesn't always work in our favor, especially when it comes to areas like friendships. We like to be surrounded by people, will do more than we should for some, and are taken advantage of at times. Because we are so busy trying to entertain and please a number of people, we may overlook the opportunity to develop quality relationships.

Clothing

Type-A's will buy stuff on sale so that we can have more, whether or not it's what we want or need. It's very hard for a Type-A to walk away from a deal. They say that people buy for two reasons: a sense of loss, or a fear of missing out. Type-A's resonate with this immensely. We also find it hard to buy something without the opinion of another, but a sale makes it easier to do so.

Residence

Our homes are our dens. We take pride in having everything in its place.

Don't get me wrong, we don't spend hours scouring our den daily, but we do like order. Extreme Type-A's set up systems in their homes where things are numbered and or labeled. We don't like others in our kitchens to help because we have systems that need to be respected and we find it difficult if others sway off track. The clutter of our place feels like a clutter of our minds, it can send us into a tailspin. There can be a junk drawer where things without a direct purpose can go but it needs to be out of sight.

Cooking

When cooking or making meals, we have the tendency to either use every pot and dirty the entire kitchen or wash and put things away as we go. There doesn't seem to be a middle road here for us. It depends on the meal and the mood we are in. We can't sit and have a sandwich unless the ingredients that we've removed from the fridge have all been put away. When preparing a meal, we cook like we are expecting a dozen, even if we are only two.

Chores

When doing chores around our home, we start several at the same time without realizing. I can start vacuuming and the next thing I know I'm putting dishes away and then I somehow move onto making the bed. We eventually get them all done; more done than we had intended on initially.

The speed at which we do these things makes Type B's heads spin. By the time they've thought about what needs to be done, we Type-A's are finished and have already moved onto something else.

Conversing

Having conversations with Type-A's can be a bit frustrating. We start telling a story and stop mid-sentence to change gears, expecting our listener to follow along. Or we will blurt something out that's been rolling around in our minds from a day or so ago and expect that we'll be understood. During a deep conversation, we might notice the beauty of a tree or sky and feel it necessary to voice our delight.

Irritants

Twist ties, knots, sauce packets, protective seals, can all send us into a real tizzy. Anything requiring the need for us Type-A's to slow down and use small motor skills seems terribly difficult.

Irritants are everywhere; I have to talk about these two:

A. Stop lights

Who invented stoplights with the flashing hand counting down, showing you how many seconds you have before it's yellow? Wow, what a stressor. We have to get through that light and will speed up accordingly to make it in time. Even more stressful is when we aren't the one driving and our driver doesn't notice this, or we're behind a driver that's not particularly plugged in.

Comparably, when driving down a busy highway we know exactly what our next move will be based on the speed of the others. We'll accelerate to stay ahead of the car behind us and to not get stuck behind the car we're approaching. Our brains are constantly mapping and re-mapping our course of action far in advance of executing it.

Road rage is very natural for Type-A's. We see the merges ahead, make the almost-red stop lights, and notice the person at the crosswalk; all at the same time without missing a beat. So, when others do not, we become flustered culminating in a fist-shaking, finger-giving kind of fury. Which of course is always fun, especially when you almost always end up at the next light with the one you've recently raged on.

B. Line ups

What an incredible waste of time and a very regular thing now due to COVID-19! The year 2020 has had me driving all around town to try and beat the line ups only to realize the time and money spent driving around was more than if

WE'RE NOT CRAZY, WE'RE TYPE A

I'd stood and waited. Does that mean I've learned from my impatience and tackle lines now? Nope, don't think so.

CHAPTER 5: LIFE PHASES

I'm now going to walk you through the different phases of my life and how I believe my Type-A personality showed itself in each one. This will lead me to discuss the point in which my health was being impacted and where my quest to become healthier began.

Childhood

Childhood is a time in your life when you should be carefree, at ease, and not riddled with emotions.

As a Type-A, this is impossible. I remember having anxiety around my inability to fall asleep as early as age 5. I wouldn't have been able to put words to it at the time, I just knew I laid in bed at night afraid that I wouldn't fall asleep which undoubtedly kept me awake and in a state of worry.

I also remember acting out so that I'd get the attention I craved. I would be the clown of the class so my "friends" would laugh.

Early on, I was labeled as the bad kid. The bully with a big mouth. I didn't want to be the bad kid. I had so much going on in my head and my body that I was not able to control, thus I acted out to get the attention I needed.

Nowadays, these children are tested for ADHD, which I was diagnosed with later in life. During my childhood though, there was no effort to understand us; instead, we were given punishments, detention, grounding, additional rules to follow, or the removal of physical activity, and the list goes on.

My child who was diagnosed with ADHD had a very different experience. I'm elated to know that there are now options for those of us that simply can't control the actions that are considered unacceptable in social situations.

Having lived with it my whole life and being medicated for a short time as an adult, I am not a fan of medication. They inhibit or change our natural drive and we don't get the chance to learn how to live with our traits. The message is that we are unable to manage them as we are, so we should change them.

Funny story about our inability to control our actions. My ADHD child joined the military. One of his trainings simulated what it would be like to lay face down in a combat field for hours. This was absolutely impossible for my boy. As he lay there, involuntary noises were coming out of his mouth. Zip, zip. Wamp, wamp. When the commander spoke harshly, it took him a moment to realize that he was doing this. It was instinctive rather than intentional.

I had the pleasure of going through some ADHD behavior modification training with my son. I wanted to try all available methods in advance of giving him medication. In grade two, we saw an incredible improvement in his actions. By keeping a daily journal where he got to remark on the good things he had done, the attention he needed was being fulfilled.

Adolescence

The bad kid! Still misunderstood. Did my parents, teachers and so-called friends think I enjoyed getting in trouble all the time? Was I just cut out to be bad? Should they give up on me?

Indeed, the acting out continued. Up the age, up the ante. It wasn't long before I found "grown-up" things were fun and very wrong which, of course, made them more interesting to me. I was 10 when I smoked my first cigarette, and 12 when I smoked my first joint. I would hang out with older boys, lie to my parents, miss curfew, and the list goes on. The thing is, I would always get caught. As a Type-A, I am unable to tell a [believable] lie. Our lies generally turn into elaborate stories that are difficult to remember. We get caught up in them every time.

At this point in my life, I could tell my dad a lie and he'd tell me exactly what it was I had done. It used to drive me crazy!

At the age of 15, my parents thought it was best if they moved us into the city. Their thought was they'd take me away from the bad crew and join an upper-echelon golf club so I'd meet children that knew how to behave. That certainly backfired! I was still the same kid, so the kids I attracted were cut from the same cloth. They loved the idea of new stock in their group. With access to what the city now had to offer, I was involved in even more "adult" stuff.

New year, new school, not a new me. Off to grade 10 where I missed more classes than I attended. I was grounded and ran away multiple times. Teetering on a path of no return. I finally got a break that I will be forever grateful for. In grade 11, my parents sent me to an all-girl private school. I was livid at the time, but it certainly helped me turn things around. This was a big expense for them. I'm guessing that they knew the cost of hiring a lawyer or the grief of losing me would be worse.

Adulthood

It took me a very long time to come to grips with who I was. From the time I was 12 until I was 46, I abused substances, both legal and non-legal, to try and quiet my mind.

There was a short reprieve from this when I first had my

children, and my mom was still alive. I felt fulfilled spending time with them without the requirement for substances. I thought I had all I needed.

However, before my daughter turned one, my mom got sick and died of a brain tumor. This event spun me back out of control for a few years. This time, it was different. I managed my days as needed with my children, put them to bed, and ventured out to null my feelings. This time, my health started to decline. I knew I was heading down a dark hole and needed to address it. So, I did what I knew to do, and went the tried and trusted route of western medicine. The outcome of this is shared in detail later when I discuss my current health quest.

Middle life

Work, children, trying to keep up with the Joneses. I had a very demanding career that I was succeeding at. I needed to be number one at all costs. I didn't know any other way. The requirement to travel, work late and participate in a work hard play harder lifestyle was mine to conquer. I did with grandeur. I was proud of my accomplishments but never felt like it was enough. I often focused more on the few losses I had rather than all the wins. At the pace I was going, even western medicine was unable to support my lifestyle.

My desire to be perfect and need to numb my pain started to take its toll. I was faced with a decision to make. I didn't want to make medicine my food, so I had to figure out how to make food my medicine. I started on a pursuit towards a healthy, medicine-free life. I knew at that time that I had my work cut out for me since I had been on pills for heartburn, sleep, constipation, anxiety, depression, and panic attacks for several decades.

CHAPTER 6: HEALTH QUEST

Health is what we all ultimately want; however, we sometimes confuse health with vanity. We often feel bad for so long we forget what it feels like to really feel great!

Earlier in life, my priorities were all about how I looked. As my health continued to deteriorate, I knew I needed to re-evaluate.

I'll walk you through my journey to wellness. Where I believe it began and where I am now. I will then provide you with some simple tips that may be able to help.

I knew I was walking on thin ice by burning the candle at both ends. I was about to crash and burn. Fortunately, my perfectionism kicked in. I needed to learn more about the impacts my lifestyle was having on my health. I knew I could make a difference and had to start somewhere.

Are you beginning to have small irritations? Heartburn? Insomnia? Constipation? Or have you already progressed to bigger concerns like anxiety? Panic attacks? Depression? Perhaps you are currently suffering from a disease? Do you know many top leading functional medical doctors suggest 80% of chronic illness is caused by inflammation due to unhealthy lifestyles and diets? Genetics will load the gun and your lifestyle will pull the trigger.

Speaking of diets… How many have you tried? Cabbage soup diet, Keto, Beach Body, diet pills, skinny teas, Simply for Life, or Weight Watchers? I've done them all and then some from as early as age 15. All reflected by weight, how I thought I looked dictated how I felt.

I used to convince myself that nothing tasted as good as feeling thin felt. Therefore, I didn't eat to be healthy; I ate or didn't eat foods based on what was considered good and bad for weight. To this day, I still need to be mindful of not obsessing with my weight and make my journey about health.

Dieting, as unhealthy as it can be, also requires willpower which is not an infinite resource. I believe, if you've used it all up when young, it escapes you in your older years. Throughout your life, if you dieted regularly, you also messed with your metabolism making it even more difficult when trying to maintain a healthy weight (which comes in all shapes and sizes!). Although obesity is definitely not healthy, neither is being too thin or abusing food, diets, exercise, or pills to attain a particular weight.

The weight scale has way too much power over us. We will allow it to decide on the type of day we are going to have, whether or not we feel good or are ready to give up on ourselves. Type-A's, it is not a competition, throw the darn scale out!

For me, eating habits coupled with drinking and smoking led to the start of many digestive issues, heartburn being the first. Off to the doctor, I went, and I was diagnosed with acid reflux and prescribed what half of the world is on, any derivative of Zantac. Doctors are trained to prescribe medication to help ease the struggles of their patients. As patients, we don't really know the questions to ask. Years later, I found out that Zantac almost completely neutralizes the acid in your stomach. This acid, which can be as strong as car battery acid, becomes neutral like vinegar. How can your stomach digest your food and get those much needed nutrients now? This can lead to even bigger problems, for example, stomach cancer.

Even with these small creeping health issues, I assumed I was healthy. I mean, fitness instructors are healthy, right? When you attend a class, you assume that they live the kind of life you'd like to mirror. As I became more involved in fitness, my bubble was partially broken around that area. I realized that this was sometimes a fallacy. At the conventions I attended to get my CECs (continuing education credits), I was astounded to see how many actually partied all night and took ephedrine to function the next day. It's sold by some supplement centers to enhance a trainer's workout. It used to be the substance found in cold medication that was being blamed for heart conditions. It speeds up your heart, opens your airways, and gives you more energy. It was never intended to be used so that you could burn the candle at both ends. Which was exactly what I found myself doing. Abusing this substance to party, work, instruct, repeat. Little did I know, I was messing with my central nervous system. Eventually, I got insomnia. I once again did what any normal person would do, and I went to the doctor. I didn't discuss my use of these pills or ask questions about how they may be impacting my sleep. I just asked for something to help. Sleeping pills were offered. How was I to realize at the time the damage I was doing to myself? I thought at that point that I had it all figured out. I could have the best of both worlds if only I took more pills. There I was in my early 40's taking heartburn medication, ephedrine to get me going, and ending my day with sleeping pills to try and shut it all off. This too started to catch up on me. Sleeping pills don't continue to work if you take them all the time. I was once again lying awake at night and panic attacks began. My days were getting longer, and I was finding it harder to function.

I was finally coming to the realization that my body was telling me something. It was time I listen to it or continue to fight it and be ready to accept the consequences. I was going to end up with a chronic illness with lifelong implications.

It was at the age of 46 that I decided to take back my health. I needed to understand what was really going on. The positive traits of being a Type-A kicked in. I wasn't going to accept all the issues that were arising. I was going to find out why. I was conveniently served up an ad on Facebook by a health coach that spoke to me: "Brain fog? Gas? Heartburn and indigestion? Feel the need to nap most afternoons? Why not detox your body and your mind." I was intrigued, so I decided to pay the money and see where it took me. The intention was to do a 10-day whole food plant-based cleanse. How hard could it be? By day 6 my head was pounding, I was nauseous, weak, and ready to give up. It was the first time in years that I'd gone six days without any substance. I remember my daughter told me, "Mom, you're worth this, don't give up on yourself.". By the end of day 7, I was a new woman. Energy to spare. Clear minded. No digestion issues. All of the things I believed I had to medicate myself for. All of the difficulties that came on from being a Type-A.

Experiencing this firsthand you'd think I'd want to live my life within those new-found confines, right? Well now, what's the fun in that? No Type-A ever does what makes most sense all the time, we prefer to challenge, challenge, challenge.

This cleanse did, however, set me on a path of wellness discovery. I wanted to know more. I pushed to learn what lifestyle I could adapt that would address my health but still allow me to enjoy some of life's less healthy pleasures. This ultimately led me to enroll in the Health Coaching program at IIN, the Institute of Integrated Nutrition. I decided to become a health coach. I now seek out opportunities to offer my experience and newfound knowledge to those suffering from similar lifestyles as me.

CHAPTER 7: RETIREMENT

Although only early in my retirement, I, like a good Type-A would, have an opinion on it.

It's upon retirement that we finally realize that our health really is our wealth. We work hard our whole lives to make enough money to retire, often overlooking our health. This is especially true of Type-A's. It's often more about how we look than feel until we can no longer ignore how we feel.

My hand was a bit forced to retire from a career I loved at the age of 55. What does a healthy Type-A do with themselves when retired so young? Why, amongst many other things, write a book of course! Albeit a tough task for a Type-A since our attention span is very short. But with all the time in the world, I decided it was a task I was going to succeed at.

CHAPTER 8: TIPS TO LIVE & LOVE IT

Living and loving life as a Type-A

I'd like to be able to tell you that I'm now 100% happy with the person that I am, but I cannot. I don't believe that is possible for a Type-A. We will challenge the status quo until the day we die. What I am, however, is very aware. I know now and understand why I feel the way I do about most things in my life. I'm much more accepting of the person I am. I ask for what I need. I openly share my weaknesses and celebrate my strengths. Allowing me to live more often in peace and harmony than ever before.

Acceptance

There seem to be several books and blogs about how to recover from being a Type-A or on changing your Type-A personality. I don't want to change who I am, how hard would that be? I choose, and recommend, acceptance. Yes, we have struggles in life. Some may even seem insurmountable, but it's all in the way you perceive it.

Manifestation is very real. If we choose to focus on the negative traits we have and allow ourselves to become consumed with them, they will manifest. However, if you accept them all, even the ones you'd prefer not to have, you will find peace with most. Being open and vocal will help with acceptance. Share with those that want to be in your life. If they choose not to accept the more trying traits, then they don't deserve to benefit from the wonderful ones.

Take 5

Teach yourself to stop, take five breaths and notice all that is around you. Type-A's are so focused on the goal that we often miss so much of the journey. It's an undertaking for a Type-A to physically stop in their tracks, remark on something around them and take 5 diaphragmic breaths before moving on to the next task. I challenge you to do this at least 3 times a day. It will make a difference in how you feel. Additionally, you will start to appreciate things in your life that have always been there, but you were always too focused on something else to notice them.

Challenge perfectionism

Work to replace being perfect with perfect moments by learning to celebrate all wins, big and small. Find perfectionism throughout your day, for example, the glory of the sun, the changing fall leaves, putting a smile on someone's face, singing loudly to your favorite song. We can wallow in our inability to be perfect, which doesn't even exist or celebrate everything that is. I'm not suggesting that we don't strive to be the very best we can be. I am suggesting that we keep the demands on ourselves in check so that those perfect moments don't go unnoticed.

Be present

Focus on the now and leave the past where it is. What's done is done! Spending countless hours rehashing something that is in the past is a complete waste of time – which, you may recall, is one thing a Type-A hates to do. Think it through and write out the lesson learned. If necessary, make a pact with yourself to handle it differently should it arise again, or celebrate how you dealt with it at the time and move on. Wallowing in the past robs you of the present and what you could accomplish in the future. Instead, chalk it up to experience and tuck it away in a reconsider-for-future-use file and leave it alone.

Choose your career wisely

Be mindful of the career you choose – you may already be working in a field that further aggravates your personality traits. Obviously, employment is necessary so you can't just quit until you find what it is that works for you. You can, however, carve out moments in your day to focus entirely on what makes you tick.

Consider being a mentor at your workplace. It gives you brownie points for being a team player and also fills your need for exterior accolades.

If you work a desk job, develop a routine that gives you a brain break at least twice during your work shift. I recommend you find a buddy and commit to a lunchtime ritual that will get you moving, ideally outdoors, and talking about something that makes you happy. If you can't find a buddy, pop in your headphones and get to walking and singing.

Bring lots of healthy energy-giving snacks. Although the vending machine is easier, it will also sabotage your emotions. Blood sugar crashes are super hard on anyone and anxiety-provoking on Type-A's.

If you are just starting your career, seek out other Type-A's for advice. Find a career that you can excel at and that makes you feel good about yourself or you will be committing to a life of displeasure and self-medication to cope.

Exercise

I can't say this enough. Type-A's need to shut their minds down. Intense exercise does this. Team sports are great, and if that's your jam, by all means! Know, however, they still play on our need to win, eliminating the complete brain break we need.

Though light exercise is also good, Type-A's may notice

that it is not intense enough and our brains will dominate. Rather than turning it off we spend time thinking about all the things we need to do. Should you choose to walk, pick a challenging course with hills, listen to music or walk with a friend having light, happy conversations.

If finding a way to commit to exercise is your issue, as was mine, become an instructor. Then you have to be present to teach. You have to give your all. You get a ton of satisfaction and make it a part of your routine. Once you've done this, it makes it really hard to step away. You feel the benefits it brings and really miss it if your schedule changes. This will make sure you are committing to exercise for the right reasons – to achieve health and free your mind.

Take responsibility for your health

Given half a chance, our bodies will thrive. Stress has a huge impact on our health and is something that Type-A's deal with regularly. We have choices to make when it comes to how we feel.

Our bodies will tell us when something isn't right. We can either listen to it or deal with the illnesses that arise. We may get a chronic stress-related disease should we not address it when the symptoms are minor. Heartburn, indigestion, constipation, headaches, anxiety, and even depression are our bodies' way of telling us that it is undernourished and overstressed. If we are rushing through everything we do, including eating, our bodies are not able to ascertain what's good and what's not, making it impossible to properly pull the needed nutrients from our food. Or if we are not eating the proper nutrients, our health will be impacted. Should we decide to trust in the western medicine route without asking questions or addressing our lifestyle, there will be negative implications.

We are responsible for our own health. Yes, sometimes disease takes hold even when we managed our lifestyles properly, however, you'll be much stronger to deal with it and more likely to have a better outcome if healthy. For me,

I want to feel good while I'm here. I know a healthy lifestyle doesn't guarantee a longer life, but I can tell you firsthand it does provide for one that feels better. I'm striving to be medicine free 'til I'm 93. (That's coming from a gal that was on a mocktail of pharmaceuticals as well as recreational substances most of her life). I believe we can achieve health and still have our guilty pleasures along the way. I have no intention of depriving myself. As mentioned, willpower is not an infinite resource. With a little education, preparation, and desire you too can live a healthy happy lifestyle. Practice the Pareto principle, the 80/20 rule. 80% of the time eat plant forward whole food that has been minimally or not at all been tampered with by man. The other 20% your body can deal with. It truly doesn't have to be all or nothing. In fact, all or nothing usually sets us up for complete failure.

I still have my sweets, snacks, and glasses of wine. In keeping with my health quest, I now try to search for ones that use natural sources where possible. I have found so much yumminess in natural food. We live in a time where selection is at its best. You do however need to ask enough questions to understand the difference between the games that the diet industry play and what truly is a good choice to make. Learn to read labels and don't settle for less.

The last point I'll make about this is to make the time for your health. You can either have food as your medicine or you will make medicine your food. I know we are all busy. Life has a way of getting ahead of us. I also know we will prioritize what's important to us. I will not scrimp when it comes to my food. I buy what I know will best serve me.

Find a way to carve out a few hours a week to prepare a healthier version of the foods you love. Seek out health-conscious cooks, like Oh She Glows, for ideas. Spend a few hours with a health coach at a grocery store tour to learn about the foods that truly are the better choices. Once you have, your body will thank you and you'll not want to feel the way you once did ever again.

Control your alcohol intake

This is a tough one for me. I know I will pay the price should I decide to drink. This is generally the case for those who drank without moderation most of their early adult life. Alcohol messes with your central nervous system and throws most cycles off track. It interferes with your sleep, causes constipation, increases anxiety, and can even play a large role in depression. We all know alcohol is a depressant, right? It sure doesn't feel like that when we are in the droves of getting a good buzz on.

Type-A's don't drink only to be social; we also drink to escape. It allows us to shut off the hamster wheel for a short while. It does catch up on us though and when it does, you too will experience a similar health quest like mine.

On the other hand, trying to abstain from anything when you are Type-A encourages obsession. If we, or someone else tells us we can't have something ever again, then we become consumed by it.

I remember one visit I had with psychologist number 33 (not really sure of the number, it felt more like 333). After a short chat about how I was doing, she looked me straight in the eyes and told me I had to quit drinking. I thought to myself "No shit, Sherlock!". That was easier said than done when spiraling out of control from grief, stress, and ill-being. At the time, it seemed to be my only escape route from an otherwise very intolerable life. I went to the psychologist that day looking for a lifeline. For her to simplify my problem by suggesting I just needed to quit drinking infuriated me. Suffice it to say I couldn't leave her office quick enough. I squashed the need for help and continued on with my toxic lifestyle. I wasn't about to have someone make me feel worse than I already did about myself.

The approach I already discussed around making deals with myself is the one I've been most successful at. Additionally, I surround myself with others that don't drink excessively. If I put myself in situations where alcohol is inevitable, I have a game plan that typically includes having a few quick drinks to get that buzzy feeling I'm looking for and then turning to soda water. I don't feel pressured by my peers and I end up sober before the evening is over so that my sleep and anxiety levels are kept in check.

There are times I will avoid certain situations and/or people if I know it's going to throw my healthy lifestyle off track. I'm not good as a bystander. I've realized that if I'm at a party I want to be in the flux of the party. I want to be the one that's doing a lot of the entertaining and silliness that comes from drinking too much. I don't believe this is as expected from me by others as it is by myself. It's an innate nature of Type-A's. I can say that I've mellowed with age and this is no longer as big a deal for me as it once was, but it still plays a role in my social life for sure.

I'm always working towards a balanced, healthy lifestyle. It does not include obsessing and worrying about what I can and cannot do but rather how I can be at peace with it all. That being said, I make decisions on how and when and what to accept and what to let go.

You need to decide what "healthy" means to you and make changes that will lead you towards this vision before you're forced to make them. It's an all-around better scenario when you make the decision rather than have something decided for you.

CHAPTER 9: RAISING A TYPE-A CHILD

I have had the great fortune of raising two beautiful and healthy children, one of which has the curse/blessing of being almost exactly like me, only the male version. When my journey began, I had no idea I was a Type-A and what that entailed. Nor did I understand that he too was a Type-A, and that his journey was just beginning. Now that I've been searching to understand the impact it's had on my life, I can so resoundingly see the traits that my boy inherited from me.

One of the hardest things a parent experiences is sitting back and allowing their children the chance to learn by their own mistakes. You see them going down the same scary path you did and want to help but you can't. It certainly makes you reflect on what you put your parents through. It is especially sad if they are no longer here for you to thank them for their continued love and support that eventually put you on the right path.

Type-A's have some traits that get in the way of being the mother we always dreamed we would be. However, there are also a lot of amazing traits that we pass along. For example, grit, determination, compassion, and loyalty. The magic would be if we knew how to feed these traits at a young age so that the overwhelming desire to garner negative attention didn't become such a large part of their make-up.

As with me, acting out and creating havoc, especially in supposedly quiet organized settings, was the norm for my boy. If he wasn't stimulated physically or mentally all of the time, then he found ways to be. The ability to be quiet and focus on one thing was completely out of his control. Being who I am only further engrained these traits.

As early as grade two, I was being encouraged to put my son on medication for ADHD. It's here that I'm grateful that I too am a Type-A because I wanted answers on alternative solutions. I was on board with considering medication if it got to the point where his actions were an obvious harm to himself. First, I wanted to try behavior modifications. I learned of one centered around positive reinforcement. Catch him doing something right. This was totally counter-intuitive to what I had seen my whole life. I simply got the wooden spoon if I was bad. Which I can now say is not a way you will foster improved actions from a Type-A. We simply find ways to accept and control the negative situation without reactions.

I was pleasantly surprised to see the improvement when we implemented a journal focusing on my son's positive actions. This gave him the attention he needed so he didn't act out for negative attention. However, in a learning environment where there is the potential of several children similar to my boy, the school didn't have the manpower to ask for these additional requirements of their staff. The journal ceased to be used and the acting out resumed.

These were my earliest memories of my attempt to help my Type-A child. I didn't knowingly label him this or try to understand what it meant until much later in my life. What I did see was years of similar actions to my own. Substance abuse, inability to be alone, remaining in unhealthy relationships, misfit careers, self-sabotage, and near-miss situations that could have had lifelong implications.

Although terrified I still do my best to support him believing he's figuring it out. All I can do is watch from the sidelines and wish I could save him from these trying, confusing, experimenting years.

CHAPTER 10: CHILDRENS FEEDBACK

Being raised by a Type-A mom

This is an unedited chapter written by my children with their point of view around life with a Type-A mom.

My son had this to say:

What was it like growing up with a Type-A mom?

If I could only use one word to describe growing up with a Type-A it is: eventful.

I consider myself very lucky to have been raised by a bit of both. Type-A and B. I would say that when you are under the wing of a Type-A mom, she always makes sure that you are stimulated because she understands the need for constant stimulation herself. There was certainly never a dull moment in our household. She always came up with activities or things for us to do to make sure we were always entertained.

I was very fortunate to get to travel with my mother over the years and she is the kind of traveler I loved being with. She could roll with the punches and live out of her suitcase or jump on a last-minute flight to Florida for the fun of it. That was the constant excitement that I needed and so did she.

Like with most Type-A personalities, I'm sure, my mom has always had a lot going on in her brain. IMPOSSIBLE to shut that thing down for 30 seconds even, which is not a negative trait but rather what helps make her so successful in all fields of her life. I would say it has taught me that slowing down sometimes is necessary to maintain our sanity.

I am 100% cut from her cloth and there is nothing I would change about the way we (TYPE-A) live our lives. It is, however, very important to acknowledge that we have a harder time shutting off or slowing down than others and require that stimulation.

My mother has taught me positive ways to channel that energy and she continues to inspire others to channel their energies through exercise and a healthy lifestyle too.

My daughter had this to say:

What was it like to be raised by a Type-A mom, you ask? Four words: Thank goodness I was. I can't imagine how different my life would be had I not been raised by a hardworking, life-loving, Type-A woman. To give you an idea of what it's like to be raised by a Type-A parent, here's a little peek into my life as my mother's daughter…

Always on the go

Growing up, my brother and I never experienced true boredom. This is because our mom kept us busy and entertained, whether that meant going out, attending events, or traveling. From Haiti to rural Nova Scotia, Mom grabbed onto every opportunity she could to allow us to see the world and have different experiences. I recall one late afternoon in April about 10 years ago, Mom and I were sitting at a library waiting for my brother to arrive when she decided the three of us would fly to Florida the next morning. She booked our trip right on the spot. To this day, I'm not sure what her reasoning was to book so impulsively. My guess? Her Type-A tendencies kicked in. They're not the type to let opportunities pass them by! More than this, being raised by a Type-A mom also meant that my brother and I never sat around the house with nothing to do. Games, cards, sports, you name it, we had it going on. As I've come to better understand my mom over time, I now look back and wonder: who was entertaining who? Mom still loves a game of cards on a Friday night.

Living life to the fullest

I've come to the conclusion that Type-A's have a hard time saying no. It's either that or they really enjoy saying yes and making things happen. From buying treats to booking vacations, it was usually "yes" with Mom. She would constantly remind us that she aspired to live her life to the fullest because "you can't spend your money when you're six feet under!". I have had incredible experiences in this lifetime due to her "giver" attitude (when warranted, of course!). Despite having multiple things on the go at any given moment, she has always committed to actively reminding herself to slow down and make the most out of every moment.

Fast pace lifestyle

Having a Type-A mom means I have learned to eat my dinner fast, put my coat on fast, and get out of the door even faster. As the child of a Type-A, I know to be ready to move quickly when I'm called. Although being rushed can cause anxiety at times, I understand that Type-A's rush not to be a bull in a china shop, but rather to get more done in the run of a day. Mom may not sit at the dinner table two minutes past dinner time, but I can assure you that she will put those few extra minutes to good use, most often putting them towards accomplishing yet another task before the day ends.

Attachment styles

An interesting part about being the child of a Type-A is the attachment style that you develop as a result. Mom has always liked having someone around her – "the more, the merrier" she believes. Due to this, we have spent and continue to spend a considerable amount of time together. Though this way of being will often help foster an incredible friendship between a parent and a child, it can also contribute to their child developing an anxious attachment style. An interesting trade-off!

Leading by example

Type-A's are hardworking by nature. Lucky for me, I've grown up watching my mom excel in her career as an executive in the sales world and most recently, as a health coach. In true Type-A fashion, Mom will work hard at something until she is the best at it. She is hungry for self-improvement and is often praised by her peers for the quality of her work. This has set an outstanding example for me and helped guide me in self-reflection about my own professional development.

Final thoughts

Despite being much different than my mom (having both Type-A and Type B traits myself), and consequently not always seeing eye to eye with her, I have grown to admire the differences between us. This book will allow us folks living with and/or loving Type-A's to better understand them.

Thank you, Mom, for this demonstration of genuine desire to help those around you.

CHAPTER 11: FINAL THOUGHTS

I've made the transition from the corporate world to focus on my passion for health coaching. I hope some of this resonated with you and gave you a few tips that may have a positive impact on your life.

If you'd like to work with me find out more at paretowellness.ca

Please know that I'm not perfect and I don't have it all figured out. I don't have total bliss in my life. I make bad decisions. I still struggle with anxiety. I fear panic attacks. I become easily irritated. I am sometimes critical of all the imperfections of my body and my life. I have too many expectations of myself and others.

However, I'm growing and learning. I'm accepting and adoring. I see and celebrate small things and moments. I smile at my mirror image. I choose to make myself happy. I like who I am. I am very proud to be medicine-free and plan to be 'til I'm 93. I understand it's a work in progress and I'm prepared to put the work in. After all, I'm worth it! Are you?